NATURE'S FREAK SHOW: UGLY BEASTS

THE BIZARRE CALIFORNIA CONDOR

BY JANEY LEVY

Gareth Stevens PUBLISHING

Please visit our website, www.garethstevens.com. For a free color catalog of all our high-quality books, call toll free 1-800-542-2595 or fax 1-877-542-2596.

Library of Congress Cataloging-in-Publication Data

Names: Levy, Janey, author.
Title: The bizarre California condor / Janey Levy.
Description: New York : Gareth Stevens Publishing, [2020] | Series: Nature's freak show : ugly beasts | Includes index.
Identifiers: LCCN 2019014320| ISBN 9781538246061 (paperback) | ISBN 9781538246085 (library bound) | ISBN 9781538246078 (6 pack)
Subjects: LCSH: California condor--Juvenile literature.
Classification: LCC QL696.C53 L48 2020 | DDC 598.9/2--dc23
LC record available at https://lccn.loc.gov/2019014320

First Edition

Published in 2020 by
Gareth Stevens Publishing
111 East 14th Street, Suite 349
New York, NY 10003

Designer: Katelyn E. Reynolds
Editor: Monika Davies

Photo credits: Cover, pp. 1, 21 Peggy Sells/Shutterstock.com; cover, pp. 1-24 (curtain background) Africa Studio/Shutterstock.com; cover, pp. 1-24 (wood sign) Rawpixel.com/Shutterstock.com; cover, pp. 1-24 (marquee signs) iunewind/Shutterstock.com; p. 5 FRAYN/Shutterstock.com; p. 7 Tim S Newman/Shutterstock.com; p. 9 JPL Designs/Shutterstock.com; p. 11 John Cancalosi/Photolibrary/Getty Images Plus; p. 13 Claudio Contreras/Nature Picture Library/Getty Images Plus; p. 15 Mark Newman/Lonely Planet Images/Getty Images Plus; p. 17 David McNew/Getty Images; p. 19 Joseph Brandt, Pacific Southwest Region U.S. Fish and Wildlife Service (https://www.flickr.com/photos/54430347@N04), Sacramento, USA/File Upload Bot (Magnus Manske)/Wikipedia.org.

Printed in the United States of America

CPSIA compliance information: Batch #CW20GS: For further information contact Gareth Stevens, New York, New York at 1-800-542-2595.

CONTENTS

Words in the glossary appear in bold type the first time they are used in the text.

THE COMMANDING CALIFORNIA CONDOR

Do you like birds? Many people do. Some have pet birds or enjoy feeding colorful wild songbirds. But the California condor is unlike any of the pet birds or wild songbirds you might know.

The California condor has been around for over 40,000 years. It's a huge bird with black feathers, wide wings, and a bare head. The condor's bare head may look frightful to some people—but that bare head serves an important purpose! You'll learn all about California condors inside this book.

STRANGE BUT TRUE!

At one time, California condors were found all over North America. Today, you can only spy one of these condors in California, Arizona, Utah, and a part of Mexico called Baja California.

AMERICAN INDIANS CALL THE CALIFORNIA CONDOR THE THUNDERBIRD.

BALD IS HEALTHY

The California condor's bare head and neck may be pink or yellowish-orange, making them stand out from their black feathers. The uncovered skin is very strange for a bird, but it's like that for a good reason.

California condors eat dead animals. As they eat, they often stick their head inside the dead animal. Rotting food—and bacteria—doesn't stick to their bare head and neck the way it would stick to feathers. And that's good for their health!

STRANGE BUT TRUE!

You might be surprised to learn the skin on an adult condor's head can also show feelings. It changes to a deep red-pink when they're courting mates or feeling stirred up.

FOR THE CALIFORNIA CONDOR, BALD IS BEAUTIFUL!

DINING ON DEAD CREATURES

California condors aren't hunters, like hawks and eagles. They're scavengers, which means they eat only carrion, or dead, rotting animals. They usually like to eat large animals, such as deer, cattle, sheep—and even whales! But they'll also eat small animals like mice and rabbits. They can hold up to 3 pounds (1.4 kg) of food in their crop, or a pouch in their **esophagus**.

Eating carrion may seem gross. But without scavengers to help clean up dead animals, think about what a mess there'd be!

STRANGE BUT TRUE!

When California condors find some tasty carrion, they eat as much as they can. They can then survive for 1 to 2 weeks without eating if they have to!

CALIFORNIA CONDORS SOMETIMES EAT SO MUCH THAT THEY HAVE TO REST FOR SEVERAL HOURS BEFORE THEY CAN FLY AGAIN.

SOARING SCAVENGERS

Do you wonder how California condors find carrion? They **soar**, or fly, high in the sky looking for their food. Their wide wings allow them to soar to 15,000 feet (4,572 m). And they can soar for hours! As they fly, they may travel 150 miles (241.4 km) a day in search of food and reach speeds of 55 miles (88.5 km) per hour.

California condors depend on their sharp eyesight to spot carrion. Their sense of smell is poor.

STRANGE BUT TRUE!

Soaring in the sky looks easy, but it takes young condors months to learn how to fly and land properly. Until they do, they often make crash landings!

THE CALIFORNIA CONDOR'S WINGS CAN REACH OVER 9 FEET (2.7 M) FROM THE TIP OF ONE WING TO THE TIP OF THE OTHER WING.

KEEPING CLEAN

Eating carrion may sound like a gross and messy action. As a result, some people think of scavengers themselves as messy birds. You might be surprised to learn California condors actually keep themselves very clean! After they eat, they rub their head and neck on grass, rocks, or branches to clean off any rotten food bits stuck to them.

California condors also take regular baths. And, they spend hours smoothing their feathers and drying them. They work hard to keep clean.

STRANGE BUT TRUE!

California condors are also lucky to have a strong immune system to keep them safe from the bacteria they come across when they dine on carrion.

CONDOR MATES AND CHICKS HELP EACH OTHER CLEAN UP.

CONDOR CULTURE

California condors are social birds that like to get together in groups. They gather when feeding, bathing, and resting. When they're together, the condors have a social order they keep using different body postures, or poses, when they **interact** with each other.

California condors often make their homes high in rocky, forested areas, such as **canyons** and mountains. They choose high places because it makes it easier for them to take off. Condors are too big and heavy to take off easily from the ground.

STRANGE BUT TRUE!

California condors don't have a real voice box like other birds do, so they can't sing or chirp. They can only make simple sounds, such as hisses.

INDIVIDUAL CALIFORNIA CONDORS KNOW AND REMEMBER EACH OTHER.

MARVELOUS MATES

Once a male and female California condor have formed a pair, they usually stay together for life. They raise their young in caves or holes in cliffs or trees. In some unusual cases, California condors may build nests made of stones and bark on dirt floors. But they usually don't build large nests for their babies.

The female condor lays just one light blue-green or almost-white egg. Both parents then take turns **incubating** the egg for around 56 days.

STRANGE BUT TRUE!

The female California condor chooses the pair's nesting spot.

IT'S HARD FOR HUMANS TO TELL MALE AND FEMALE CALIFORNIA CONDORS APART. BUT DON'T WORRY—THE CONDORS CAN TELL WHICH IS WHICH!

BRINGING UP BABY

Raising a California condor chick, or baby, takes a lot of time and work. Both parents keep the chick warm after it **hatches**. Both parents also feed their chick by **regurgitating** meat from their crops. That might sound gross, but it's important! This continues until the chick learns to pick up its own food.

The chick starts learning to fly when it's about 5 to 6 months old. It depends on its parents for at least a year, and the chick may stay with its parents for up to 2 years!

STRANGE BUT TRUE!

A chick uses its egg tooth, a sharp point on its beak, to break free of its egg. It can take a chick many days to get out!

ADULT CALIFORNIA CONDORS HAVE NO PREDATORS EXCEPT HUMANS. BUT BLACK BEARS OR LARGE BIRDS MAY ATTACK CONDOR CHICKS IN A NEST.

ENDANGERED

There's bad news about the future of California condors. They're critically endangered, or highly likely to become **extinct** in the wild.

Many reasons exist for the condors' condition. There aren't many California condors, and they **reproduce** slowly since it takes so long to raise each chick. They sometimes fly into power lines and die. Lead poisoning is also a danger caused when condors mistakenly eat bullets, or small pieces of metal shot from guns, in carrion. It's up to us to save them. Will you help?

STRANGE BUT TRUE!

California condors are considered one of the most uncommon birds in the world. In 2016, there were only 446 California condors worldwide!

HELPING THE ENDANGERED CALIFORNIA CONDOR

DANGERS	HELPING CONDORS
REPRODUCE SLOWLY	·A breeding program to produce more California condors started in 1987. All California condors were brought together in one place to reproduce so the condors wouldn't go extinct. ·Starting in 1992, some of the condors raised in captivity were let go into the wild. This program continues today!
MAY FLY INTO POWER LINES	·We can set California condors free in areas where few people live.
LEAD POISONING FROM BULLET PIECES IN CARRION	·We can catch wild condors and treat them for lead poisoning. ·We can ban lead bullets for hunting.

GLOSSARY

canyon: a deep valley with steep sides

captivity: the state of being caged

esophagus: the tube that leads from the mouth through the throat to the stomach

extinct: no longer living

hatch: to break open or come out of

immune system: the parts of the body that fight germs and keep it healthy

incubate: to keep eggs warm so they can hatch

interact: to do things with other people or animals

mate: one of two animals that come together to produce babies

regurgitate: to bring food back up out of the stomach

reproduce: when an animal creates another creature just like itself

soar: to drift in the air without moving wings up and down

FOR MORE INFORMATION

BOOKS

Dunn, Mary R. *California Condors.* North Mankato, MN: Capstone Press, 2015.

Sabelko, Rebecca. *California Condors.* Minneapolis, MN: Bellwether Media, 2019.

Waxman, Laura Hamilton. *California Condors: Wide-Winged Soaring Birds.* Minneapolis, MN: Lerner Publications, 2016.

WEBSITES

California Condor
animals.sandiegozoo.org/animals/california-condor
Learn more about California condors on this site.

California Condor
peregrinefund.org/explore-raptors-species/California_Condor
Find information about California condors as well as lots of photos on this website.

California Condor
fws.gov/sacramento/es_kids/CA-Condor/
Discover some interesting facts about California condors and how to help them here.

Publisher's note to educators and parents: Our editors have carefully reviewed these websites to ensure that they are suitable for students. Many websites change frequently, however, and we cannot guarantee that a site's future contents will continue to meet our high standards of quality and educational value. Be advised that students should be closely supervised whenever they access the internet.

INDEX